THANK GOODNESS
WE BOTH HAVE OUR
SOFT SIDES

Published by Sellers Publishing, Inc.

Copyright © 2020 Sellers Publishing, Inc.
Illustrations © 2020 Sophie Corrigan

Sellers Publishing, Inc.
161 John Roberts Road, South Portland, Maine 04106
Visit our website: www.sellerspublishing.com ● E-mail: rsp@rsvp.com

Charlotte Cromwell, Production Editor

ISBN 13: 978-1-5319-1218-5

10 9 8 7 6 5 4 3 2 1

Printed in China.

THANK GOODNESS WE BOTH HAVE OUR SOFT SIDES

Illustrated by

SOPHIE CORRIGAN

SELLERS
PUBLISHING

We would both like
our relationship to be
just ducky.

But if I said things
were always perfect . . .

you might say I was lion.

Rhino I can be
hard to take
at times.

I horse around a lot.

I have some habits
that bug you.

AAAAAAAAAAAAAAA

I say things that
get your goat.

Sometimes I badger you.

I axolot of
silly questions . . .

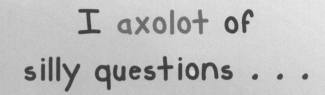

Or ask for
squid-pro-quos.

We can get so
tangled up in
our feelings
and emotions.

We sometimes lose sight
of what matters most . . .

our love for each otter.

It's hugely important
that we remember all
the special times
we've shared.

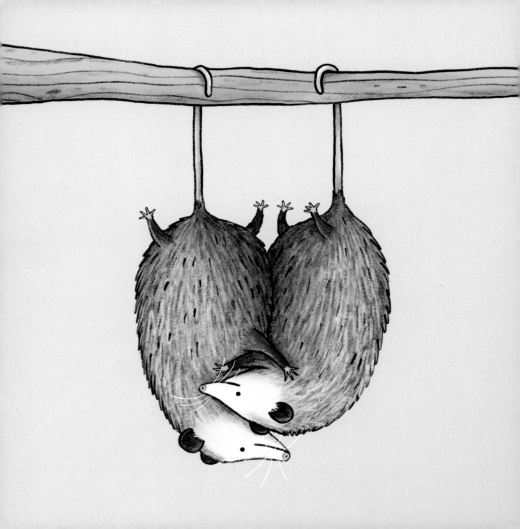

You are possumbly
the most amazing thing
that's ever happened
to me.

I spent so much time looking . . .

for some bunny like you.

Someone whose goals
and values dovetail
with my own.

Someone who speaks
the truth instead
of just puffin.

When I met you,
I knew right away I hit
the jackpot pig time!

I was so hoppy!

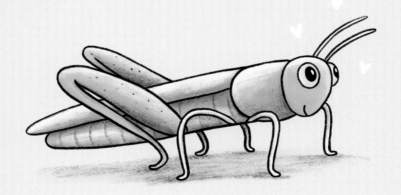

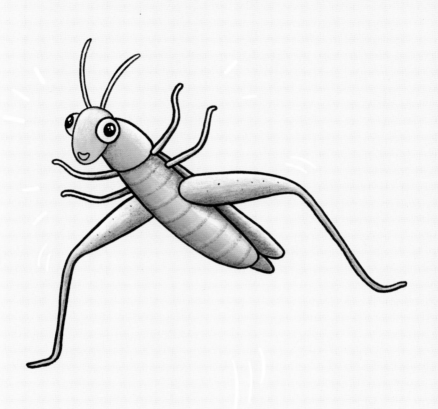

I could bear-ly contain my excitement.

It was love
right from the gecko.

I will never frog-et
how meeting you changed
my life.

You give it porpoise
and meaning.

So, although
we may have our
ups and downs . . .

I hope we can focus
on the love that
lynx us together.

Owl always be
true to you.

And I hope ewe
will be true to me, too.

I may not be purrrfect . . .

but the felines I have for
you will never change.

I give you this book
as a way of saying
you'll always be
deer to me.

Let's seal it with a kiss.

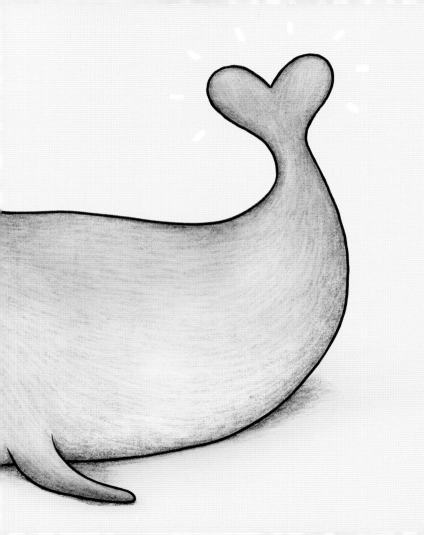